IMAGES
of England

ADWICK, ARKSEY
BENTLEY, CARCROFT
AND WOODLANDS

The original Bentley tram terminus in High Street, with a section of track leading into Chapel Street so that the vehicles would not obstruct other traffic in the main road.

IMAGES
of England

ADWICK, ARKSEY
BENTLEY, CARCROFT
AND WOODLANDS

Compiled by
Peter Tuffrey

TEMPUS

First published 1997, reprinted 2002
Copyright © Peter Tuffrey, 1997

Tempus Publishing Limited
The Mill, Brimscombe Port,
Stroud, Gloucestershire, GL5 2QG

ISBN 0 7524 0713 9

Typesetting and origination by
Tempus Publishing Limited
Printed in Great Britain by
Midway Colour Print, Wiltshire

Contents

Introduction   7

1.   Adwick   9

2.   Arksey   35

3.   Bentley   43

4.   Carcroft and Bullcroft Colliery   85

5.   Woodlands and Brodsworth Colliery   105

I would like to dedicate this book to my good friend the late Frank Shaw, an inspirational, kindly man who is not forgotten.

Introduction

Three of the featured villages, Adwick, Bentley and Carcroft, were greatly altered from their rural existences, dating back centuries, into sprawling mining communities with the sinking at the early part of the century of the Bentley, Brodsworth and Bullcroft Collieries. Indeed, a whole new village, a 'model' one no less, was created, and named Woodlands, to accommodate the miners working at Brodsworth Colliery. While Arksey lay in the shadow of Bentley Colliery, it remained relatively unscathed by colliery developments.

The villages in this book follow each other alphabetically and, within each village section, photographs of a similar character are grouped together ie: street scenes, formal groups, mining scenes and traders. Quite a range of different pictures is included, featuring floods, a man dressed as half bride/half soldier, carnival cavalcades and posing miners.

The Adwick-le-Street pictures show that the area was once rather quaint and charming, though while familiarising myself with its various features before writing the captions, I was struck by how little remained intact and how much had been altered unsympathetically. Many of the Adwick photographs are from the collection of the late Frank Shaw, to whom I have dedicated this book. Indeed, his widow Sheila, and son Andrew were kind enough to let me consult his notes for help with the caption writing. Frank and myself, along with another picture collector 'Lol' Freeman, were regular visitors to postcard fairs and it was there where he collected a good few pictures, besides the ones he obtained locally. Before his untimely death, Frank was actually working on an Adwick book of his own, so I am pleased to have adapted the bare bones of that for inclusion here. The one picture from Frank's Adwick collection that I am particularly fond of is the Adwick Hall print. How splendid this one-time home of the Washingtons must have appeared in its day. The bulk of the Adwick pictures show no other forms of transport than horses and carts and railways. When peeping at the current dilapidated condition of the old railway station, it is difficult to imagine that this building was formerly a contender in the region's Best Kept Station Competition.

The main feature of the Arksey section is, without doubt, the floods ably captured by the Doncaster-based Empire View photographic company. Whilst Arksey Hall is no longer the house of a local squire, it nevertheless survives intact and has a useful function, currently being a nursing home.

A number of the Bentley pictures are from the collection of Gordon and Mary Bower and I am grateful for their help over the years. The ones of the colliery under construction were taken by Luke Bagshaw and are notable for their clarity. By looking at newspaper references while researching the Bentley section, I was surprised by the acute housing problems caused by the vast influx of miners at the colliery. Workers were paying rent for houses even when only the foundations were laid, so desperate was the problem. Quite a few articles also regularly appeared about the state of Bentley's tram track, difficulties finally being resolved with the introduction of trolleybuses. Probably the most curious picture in the Bentley section shows children posing with a policeman. During a school strike, parents wishing their children to attend school were escorted there by a huge 'bobby'.

Given that mining is a hazardous job, the area was not without its share of tragedies, and the most moving picture in the Bentley section, if not the entire book, shows the open grave of miners killed in the Bentley pit disaster.

For the Carcroft and Bullcroft Colliery section, I have used more of Frank Shaw's pictures and notes, which are augmented with some interesting information discovered in the local newspapers. Miners posing in the early days of colliery operations reveal to me some gritty portrait studies, besides giving a glimpse into the poor working conditions.

One of my personal favourites in the Woodlands and Brodsworth Colliery section is the picture of the sod cutting ceremony. I like this not only for the large number of interesting faces all peering at the camera, but for the different age ranges revealed. It might not have been assumed that young children would have a place in this event. Yet, they are to be seen posing as proudly and as full of hope for the colliery as landowner Charles Thellusson himself (left of the wheelbarrow).

The last few photographs at the end of the book - scenes from Woodlands carnivals - show the patience and skills of photographer Edgar Leonard Scrivens when depicting children, probably spending an infinite amount of time organising their poses.

As previously stated, the book is largely concerned with depicting areas as they changed into sprawling mining communities. Now that all three collieries have gone, each village is probably awaiting the next development, in whatever form it may appear.

One
Adwick

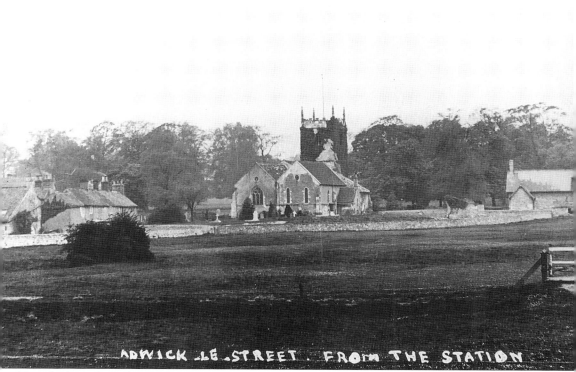

View looking from the station, towards St Lawrence's church, Adwick. The original village of Adwick, centred on Village Street, was mentioned in the Domesday Book. Whilst having a rural population of just over 300 at the turn of the century, this increased considerably, into the thousands during the ensuing years. The opening of the Brodsworth and Bullcroft Collieries brought an industrial era that entirely altered the character of the district. Miners and their families from Nottinghamshire, Derbyshire and older coalfields, flocked to the area, attracted by the prospect of high wages in winning coal from the rich new seams.

Doncaster Road, Adwick, looking towards Carcroft, showing the thoroughfare before widening took place in 1927. Linden Cottage on the left, standing in front of the town hall, has since been demolished. Glebe Cottage, the property further along the road on the left, is still extant, though the one to the right of the large tree has been cleared. Donelly's farm buildings may be seen on the right.

Church Lane looking towards St Lawrence's church. The buildings on the immediate left formed part of Mrs Biddie's farm. A notice on one of them mentions the name of 'H. Greenoff, Dealer'. The local trade directories show that several other members of the Greenoff family owned businesses in Adwick. To the right of the picture and north east of the church, it is thought that a moated site formerly existed.

Station View, which eventually came to be known as Planet Road. The houses have since been cleared.

A group of potential models pose on Doncaster Road, Adwick. The thoroughfare is much wider today and Ashwood House now stands on an area beyond the railings. The Adwick-le-Street Urban District Council was formed in 1915, comprising Adwick, Woodlands, Carcroft and Highfields.

Church Lane looking towards the church, with the Village Institute on the left and a row of commercial properties adjacent. The post office is situated in the corner premises on the right. At one time, early closing in Adwick was on a Thursday. Office hours for the post office were 9 am to 7 pm., closing at 1 pm on Thursdays.

Grocer, draper and off-licence holder: D. Kirkby's shop at Adwick. In this stretch of properties, which became known as Planet Road, there was another grocer and a fish and chip shop during the 1950s and 1960s.

Village Street, Adwick, featuring the school and school house, St Lawrence's church and three young boys, two of them with delivery baskets. J. Morgan Jones in *Adwick-Le-Street A Short History of the Parish Church* [1962] states that it is difficult to establish a definite date for the foundation of the present Parish church, but 1150-1200 seems a reasonable estimate for it was probably developed from an early aisleless Norman nave and chancel, the first addition being the north chapel in the thirteenth century. 'Of the original fabric there still remains the South doorway and a built up semi-circular headed window visible on the South wall of the Chancel. It is possible that the semi-circular sedilia are also part of the original Church.'

Two shops on Church Lane adjacent to the Village Institute. The shop on the left, selling confectionery, was run by Bertha Taylor. The post office is on the right with a Mr W.J. Gardiner posing in the doorway. Groceries and provisions were also sold in the post office. Bertha Taylor's shop was eventually taken over by the post office, becoming Adwick's first telephone exchange.

On the bridge near Carcroft and Adwick railway station, looking towards the church. The view was taken before the new road to Windmill Balk Lane was constructed in 1927.

A rural scene on Village Street looking towards Fern Bank Cottages, now demolished. It has been stated that Adwick generally has not got a rich historical background and, like other farming villages in the area, was pretty much the same for centuries until the advent of the collieries, namely Brodsworth Main and Bullcroft Main.

Although the caption on the postcard reads Ings Lane, the footpath, leading to Skellow, eventually became known as Planet Road. The latter originated from the Planet Trading Co. who owned a factory nearby which was later used as a fire station. The chimney in the distance belonged to the Bullcroft Colliery at Carcroft. The Adwick-le-Street and Carcroft Working Men's Club opened in two houses on Ings Lane in 1908, but moved to more commodious premises a year later.

View on Fern Bank looking towards Fern Bank Cottages. The land and farm on the right has been levelled and houses erected.

View looking from the station towards St Lawrence's church. On 8 January 1947, the *Chronicle* stated that restoration work, which had taken place at Adwick-le-Street Parish Church in connection with the recent opening of the Lady Chapel, had revealed the existence of two more tombs of the Washington family. The first of these bears a Latin inscription which reads: 'Here lies Richard Washington, Knight and Lord of Adwick, who died in his 39th year, 1678'. The second tomb appeared to be that of Elizabeth and James Washington.

View from Redhouse Lane looking down Robinson Lane, the latter becoming Fern Bank after 1910. On the left is the Methodist chapel. The row of terraced houses in the centre still bears a plaque: 'Fern Bank, 1910'. All the properties beyond these have been cleared.

A unique view taken from St Lawrence's church tower before the new road from Carcroft and Adwick station to Windmill Balk Lane was constructed. St Lawrence's Terrace may be seen on the right. The horse and cart wending its way along Church Lane in the foreground belongs to R.J. Dixon. Much of the property on the left was demolished in subsequent years.

The old mill and bridge, Adwick, captured by well known local photographer Edgar Leonard Scrivens. Apparently, the earliest plan that can be located to show the mill is a tithe map of 1844. The plan, although relatively small scale, shows the mill and adjoining mill house, a building to the north east of the mill, the stable block and two other buildings. The head race and tail race ponds are also clearly shown. Nearly a hundred years later the Ordnance Survey map of 1930 shows significant changes. The head race is shown without the pond as on earlier maps, although the retaining earthworks to the east and west of the head race can be clearly seen.

Church Lane, Adwick, looking towards the railway station with 'Domino Row' on the left. These buildings were demolished during the mid-1980s by the Sheffield demolition firm Demex.

On the left, in this view of Village Street, is Greenoff's bow-fronted shop and the Forrester's Arms public house. At one time a small fair was held in the Forrester's yard. An inn of this name on the site may be traced back to at least 1855, and at one time the Forrester's Lodge of Oddfellows used to meet on the premises. Also, at one time the Adwick Bowls Club had its headquarters in the pub. Between 1822 and 1838 the inn may have been called the Plough. The bow-fronted property on the left has been demolished and an entrance near the site now leads to Park Mews.

A view from the top of St Lawrence's church tower, looking along Village Street. On the right can be seen Old Row, New Row and the gamekeeper's cottage. The new road from Carcroft and Adwick station to Windmill Balk Lane enabled vehicles to avoid the torturous village street with its awkward turnings. The cost of the new road, including the compulsory purchase of the land, was about £7,000.

The Northern Counties Cinema Company opened Adwick's New Empire on Church Lane on 2 December 1912, with seating for 800. At the time of its closure in 1958 the premises were owned by Intimate Cinemas (Adwick) Ltd. Currently, the property houses the Stag Slax factory. All the other properties depicted have been demolished.

Carcroft and Adwick station, looking north, was built in 1859-61 on the GN & GC line, with limestone walls and a Welsh slate roof. The Doncaster to Leeds railway, running from south east to north east across the area, appears to have had little influence upon Adwick's character, which remained agricultural until the early years of the present century when the Brodsworth and Bullcroft collieries opened. The station closed to goods traffic in June 1965, and to passengers on 6 November 1967. A new station has since opened in recent years slightly south of the original site.

The staff formerly employed at Carcroft and Adwick station included a station master, a checker and four porters. At one time, few opportunites existed for women to find employment in Adwick; they had to travel to Doncaster. The *Chronicle* of 31 October 1913 reported on alterations at the station: 'At a rough estimate, 3,000 people use this station every week, yet there is only one waiting room. It is now proposed to remove the porter's cabin from the up platform to the opposite side, and in its place erect a large general waiting room. At the rear of the existing buildings is to be a transit shed, while on the opposite side will be a new ladies' waiting room.'

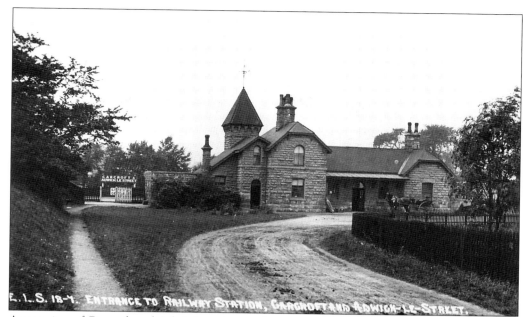

A rear view of Carcroft and Adwick station, with an entrance in the centre for those wanting to use the station's facilities. In 1945 a train carrying troops was derailed near the station, though fortunately no one was hurt.

At one time, twenty-two trains stopped daily at Carcroft and Adwick station, though passenger traffic was not heavy - as might have been expected in view of the convenient bus services which traversed the area. Nevertheless, the station in its hey-day was so smart and tidy that station master George Smeaton entered it in the LNER Best Kept Station Garden Competition.

Views of Adwick Mill and stream. An unpublished and undated manuscript held in the Doncaster MBC Reference Library states that following a search no firm date for the construction of the mill could be found. And, while the datestone on the house reads 1786, analysis of the land tax records for Adwick-le-Street revealed that the building was occupied in 1784. 'The land tax, which began in 1784, named the owner of each property together with the name of the occupier, who was not necessarily the same person. Hence for Adwick Mill from 1784 until 1789 the owner is given as Charles Duncombe and the occupier as William Boulton'.

As the Duncombe family at one time seem to have been the chief landlord in the Adwick area, it has been suggested that they instigated the building of the mill, put up the funds for its initial construction and organised the engineering of the mill dyke. Subsequent owners of the mill have included Thomas Bradford, William Barton, William Hobson, Robert Hobson, John Askham, George Askham, Peter Thellusson, Elizabeth Thellusson, Augustus Thellusson, Charles Grant-Dalton, Northern Dairies Ltd, George Newsome, Elsie Newsome, and Richard and David Martin. A newspaper advert dated 16 February 1842, for the sale of the mill, indicates that steam power had already been installed, but the original date of this remains unclear. The advert also shows that the four pairs of grinding stones in the mill were capable of grinding fifty loads per day, and that the water wheel was 'large and powerful'.

Church Lane looking towards the church and showing, at this time, the newly constructed houses on the left. The church was restored in 1862 and the chancel partially restored in 1895 by the then Rector, the Revd E.S. De Courcy Ireland. A new organ was provided at the same time and in 1904 a reredos and altar were erected by the Wightman family in memory of their parents.

Windmill Balk Lane, Adwick-le Street, probably during the early 1930s. The road has also been known as Doctor's Balk as a doctor once lived at Linden House further along the route. At one time there were some allotments on the left, but these were cleared for housing developments. A school and a library have also been built along the thoroughfare.

Police station, Windmill Balk Lane, Adwick-le-Street, looking north west. The picture house may be seen adjacent on the right. The *Chronicle* of 7 June 1912 stated: 'The first police station at Adwick-le-Street is now fast nearing completion... Provision is made for the lodging of prisoners, there being five cells, while there will also be a police officer and a house for a resident police officer. It was hoped that the building would be completed by August, but through the coal strike building operations were delayed, and it will probably be a month later when the premises are ready for their purpose'.

Children emerging from Adwick's first picture house on Windmill Balk Lane. The premises were known locally as 'Marlowe's', a gentleman of that name being the manager.

A group of children from the school on Windmill Balk Lane, Adwick, pose for the camera. The photograph was taken in the school playground.

Woodlands Road, Adwick, linking Doncaster Road with the Great North Road at Woodlands.

Doncaster Road, Adwick, looking towards Carcroft. Adwick police station is out of view to the left. Before the new road from Adwick and Carcroft station to Windmill Balk Lane was built, a survey revealed that approximately 6,500 vehicles used the old route via Village Street, over a seven day period.

Postcard view taken in the yard or garden of Linden Cottage, standing in front of the rectory. The postmark on the reverse of the postcard is 22 December 1905.

Adwick-le-Street Rectory was purchased in 1952 by Adwick-le-Street UDC to house the treasurer's department. The transfer took place in August 1954, the rest of the UDC departments remaining in the old council offices in Village Street. During the following year the new council chamber was completed and an official opening took place on 6 December 1955. A booklet published about the building to coincide with its opening as a town hall includes the following historical information: '[The building] dates back to the reign of King Charles the Second, to be precise, the year 1682... One Albrede de Lisureo gave the "glebe" of St Laurence's Church to the Nunnery at Hampole, but after the dissolution of that Order, a Mrs Anne Saville of Methley purchased it at a cost of £900 and "settled" it upon the Church forever.... The Reverend Joshua Brooke, being the incumbent and having his income considerably enlarged by the addition of [that] benefice, built at his own cost [in 1682] the present parsonage house from the foundation'. Joshua Brooke was instituted rector on 29 July 1682, remaining in office until he died in 1720.

Adwick Town Hall was purchased by Adwick-le-Street UDC in 1952 for £2,000. When reconstruction work started it was discovered that there was extensive infestation, both past and present, of Death Watch Beetle, Furniture Beetle and House Longhorne Beetle in the roof timbers and other woodwork. Consequently all timbers were removed from the old rectory and pre-stressed concrete beams and floors substituted. Archaeological excavations proved disappointing, only one shilling and one penny being discovered. The penny was dated 1770, the shilling 1817.

Photograph taken at the junction of Windmill Balk Lane and Village Street at Adwick, looking towards the police station, the twin-gabled building left of centre. Glebe Cottage is in the centre of the picture; the property adjacent to the right was once a shop. A new road from Carcroft and Adwick station to Windmill Balk Lane was opened to traffic during July 1927. Costing £7,000, 25 per cent was borne by the MOT, 25 per cent by the County Council and the remainder by Adwick Council.

View along Village Street, Adwick, with the church of St Lawrence in the distance and Park House on the right. The church, a stone building in the Norman and Early English styles, with several modern additions, has the Thelluson chapel on the northern side. In it are some altar tombs with incised slabs, dating from 1548, dedicated to the Washingtons, who were lords of the manor from the sixteenth to the eighteenth centuries. Under an arch between the chapel and the chancel there is a large tomb of an early member of the Washington family, dated 1579. It is said that the Stars and Stripes was evolved from their coat of arms.

Village Street looking towards the Forrester's Arms public house. A policeman in the centre of the picture takes time off to pose for the camera. The park to the left occupies part of the site of Adwick Hall, now demolished.

The Wesleyan chapel on Fern Bank, built in 1887, the picture dating from 1902. Another chapel formerly existed on Little Lane. Today, the Fern Bank chapel offers Sunday worship and a Sunday school. There is also a 'Bright Hour' from 2.45 pm on the first Wednesday of each month.

Interior view of the Fern Bank Wesleyan chapel.

The school and schoolhouse, complete with bell, on Village Street, Adwick. Only the schoolhouse exists today since the school was demolished in 1974. Unsubstantiated local claims allege that the buildings were erected from the ruins of Adwick Hall.

View from the junction of Windmill Balk Lane and Church Lane, Adwick. The road on the left was constructed in in 1927. Originally, objection to the scheme was made by a Mrs Atkinson, who said it meant destroying her house, by J.S. Mellor, agent for the Brodsworth Estate, who favoured an alternative road and by W. Clark, who said the proposal would make a terrible mess of his farm.

Shown here is a print of Adwick Hall, formerly the home of the Washington family for well over 200 years; after the Civil War it was confiscated and only recovered with some difficulty. It was later run as a ladies' boarding school by a Miss Simpson. The building's demise is aptly described by C.W. Hatfield in his *Historical Notices of Doncaster Vol I* (1866): 'Adwick Hall is a mass of ruins... a scene of desolation has overtaken the revered home of the late Dr Inchbald. The garden with its flowers is no more. The pump alone remains an abiding relic of a time honoured mansion. The hall is dismantled and a portion of the materials used in the erection of farm premises at Pigburn'.

A May Day parade climbing to the top of Planet Road. Kirby is the name above the shop on the left. The properties on the left were nicknamed 'Domino Row' since they were tarred black and had white window frames. All the houses and shops shown here were demolished during the mid-1980s.

A close up of Fern Bank Cottages on the left, now demolished. The road ahead leads to Adwick Mill. The small building on the right was once a cowshed. Local historian Frank Shaw mentions that Fern Bank Cottages may once have been called Fisherman's Cottages. John Magilton in *The Doncaster District An Archaeological Survey* (1977) states: 'The Village has suffered greatly from redevelopment throughout this century, although some interesting structures remain and are worth preserving'.

The *Butterfly Queen* being performed in the Empire Palace cinema on Church Lane at Adwick. The cinema, built in 1912 , now provides factory accommodation.

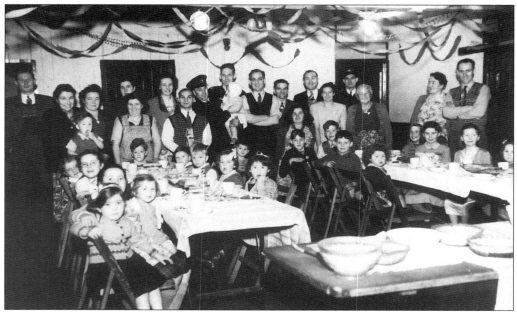

A Christmas party inside the old Planet Trading Co.'s factory which was eventually used as a fire station.

Two
Arksey

View of High Street, Arksey, looking east. Brook Villa is on the right along with the All Saints' church hall. The building off-centre to the right has been demolished, as have all those on the left. The *West Riding Directory* (1908) states: 'Arksey is a parish on the river Don and Great North Road, with a station on the main line of the Great Northern Railway, 3 miles north of Doncaster, about 35 from York and $158\frac{1}{2}$ from London... Two local quarries supply the neighbourhood with stone for repairing the roads. There are several moats and elevated mounds in the neighbourhood, probably the remains of Roman military works [including] the Roundabout near Arksey... The soil is loamy in one part and clay and limestone in others; the subsoil is gravel. The chief crops are wheat, barley, oats and turnips'.

Arksey during Floods. view from Church Tower. Empire View

Up to 6 pm on Monday 23 May 1932 Arksey streets were perfectly dry. The farmers in the district had been warned of the danger of flooding by the authorities and throughout Sunday night and Monday there was a constant stream of horses, cattle, pigs and sheep being driven to higher land at Warmsworth and Cusworth. From the top of Arksey church tower it was possible to see right across the low-lying land to Barnby Dun, from where most of the water had flooded back. On seeing the water approaching, the vicar went round the village warning everyone to remove any stock or valuable furniture into upstairs rooms.

A typical scene at Arksey during Floods.

When the water reached the village it came in a wave many feet deep, and within a few hours many of the houses were standing in 8 to 10 ft of water. The almshouses caught the full force of the floods and had to be evacuated immediately, the last resident being removed by boat at 1.30 am. The loss to poultry keepers was enormous and the bodies of hens floated past the houses.

In the deeper areas most of the houses had been evacuated, but where the water was only 2 or 3 ft deep all the upstairs windows were thronged and jokes were passed freely along about the rowing style of the amateur boatmen. An incident which caused a great deal of amusement among the residents occurred when a milkman, holding a can of milk in one hand, stepped clumsily into a boat, setting it rocking so wildly that he lost his footing and fell back with a splash into a couple of feet of water. Another milkman noted for his cycling feats under normal conditions excelled himself during the flood period. Carrying a can of milk in one hand and with only the handlebars and saddle of his cycle showing above the surface of the water, he carried on with his round and maintained a very efficient service.

The rushing water washed away a good deal of ballast from the railway lines, and all LNER main line trains between Doncaster and York were diverted after 10.30 am on Tuesday 24 May. They had to make a detour through Stainforth and Applehurst Junction, rejoining the main line a few miles north of Doncaster. The *Flying Scotsman* was somewhat delayed by having to make that detour. The only train to travel on the line during its temporary closure was a goods train carrying ballast for the repair of the embankment.

Arksey Hall had never been flooded before, but in 1932 the water covered the ground floor to a depth of 18 inches and garden frames from the grounds were found floating hundreds of yards away. A horse pulling a cattle float, conveying a number of pigs through the flooded Arksey streets, refused to move, being terrified by the depth of the water. The driver, who had only one leg, was in a dilemma, but a bystander donned a swimming costume and plunged in up to his shoulders, leading the horse to safety. One Arksey resident who was a keen bird fancier, took the whole of his stock of canaries into a bedroom and released the birds, leaving them plenty of food for a long stay. When a *Gazette* representative visited the area, the birds could be seen perched on the window ledges.

Arksey High Street was 6 ft deep in water and the greatest difficulty was experienced in rescuing the occupants of the post office. It was impossible to rescue them from the ground floor and a 20 ft ladder had to be balanced against the house side from the bottom of a small boat and down that they made a precarious escape. The water also entered the church and the vicar had to remove all valuables in the middle of the night.

Large numbers of rats took refuge in the houses and six were killed within a few minutes in one home. Many frogs could also be seen swimming about in the streets, while spawn was floating in great patches on the surface. Those people living in Arksey whose homes were not affected by the floods were cut off from Doncaster because the roadway leading to the village was flooded to a depth of of several feet, and it was only possible to cross in carts provided by the council.

Arksey Hall, a two storey cement rendered property reputedly has 'a Tudor core', according to Magilton (1977). He also adds that the hall has an internal feature dated 1653, but the remainder is probably Georgian, though the roof is modern. The porch features two Doric columns while an adjacent two storey outbuilding is probably contemporary with the final alterations to the hall in about 1820. One of Arksey Hall's noted squires was William Chadwick JP. By the mid-1960s Arksey was privately owned though divided in two, the rear portion being used by Denbigh's Cleaners as their area headquarters. Since that time, the hall has become a nursing home.

E.L.S. 64-19. THE VICARAGE, ARKSEY.

The two storey Arksey Vicarage dates from the late sixteenth or early seventeenth century, having later additions and alterations. Magilton (1977) states: 'Walls of magnesian limestone rubble, roof modern... mullioned windows, probably not original'.

Arksey All Saints' church dates from about 1150 and comprises various styles of architecture from the Transitional Norman to Late Perpendicular. It consists of chancel, nave, aisles, transept, south porch and an embattled central tower with small spire. There is a beautiful font with a cover dated 1662, a pulpit of 1634, and monuments to the family of Sir W. Cooke, bart of Wheatley. The windows display the arms of Henry (Plantagenet), Duke of Lancaster, and other heraldic glass. The church was restored during the years 1869 and 1870 under the direction of Sir G.G. Scott RA at a cost of about £3,000 which was raised by voluntary contributions. The register dates from 1559.

View from the top of Arksey church tower.

Arksey station, on the former GNR main line, closed on 5 August 1952.

Three
Bentley

Bentley's Infirmary Demonstration heading eastwards, past the Druids Arms public house, on High Street. These events were once held annually to raise funds for the Doncaster Infirmary. A number of patients were amongst the 'demonstration', which passed through the streets around the town, headed by a brass band. Children with collection boxes encouraged onlookers to make donations.

Children posing for the camera along the seemingly traffic-free Bentley Road, looking south west. The same cannot be said today. Cusworth Road is on the right while a plaque on the houses on the left reads: 'Western Cottages, 1893'.

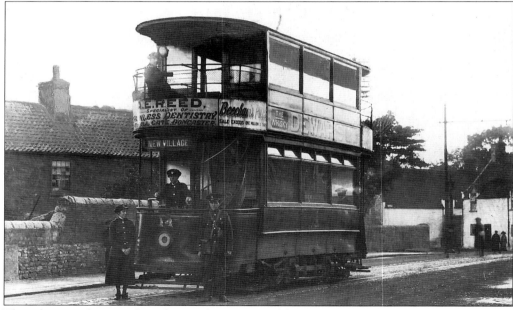

This photograph was taken during the First World War at Bentley, largely denoted by the presence of the female crew and the tram's headlamp mask, a precaution against Zeppelin raids. Four conductresses began work in July 1915 and during the following spring they all qualified as tram drivers. When they began their duties, no one knew whether to call them 'motoress', 'motorwoman', or 'driver'. Besides the difficulty of staffing the trams during the war, there was also the problem of maintaining them due to the shortage of skilled labour.

In the early years of this century people were transported to and from Bentley in horse drawn carriages, the operators including Stoppanies and Hodgson & Hepworth. The first tram arrived in Bentley on 27 October 1902. A tram driver (motorman) and conductor are pictured at the original Bentley High Street terminus which had a section of track leading into Chapel Street; a Methodist chapel may be seen in the background. Car No. 22 was purchased in 1904 and withdrawn from service in 1930.

Car No. 14 has just glided over the flood arches at the Doncaster end of Bentley Road and is pictured passing Yarborough Terrace, to the right. The vehicle was purchased by Doncaster Corporation in 1902, fitted with a top deck cover and a direct staircase in 1913, but withdrawn in 1930. The road between Bentley village and the Doncaster boundary was developed in the last two decades of the nineteenth century. Most of the dwellings are fairly modest terraced houses, but the row with the bay windows on the left, looks more substantial.

View in old rural Bentley. In an article titled 'The Development of Bentley' the *Chronicle* reported on 25 February 1910: '[Bentley] within the past few years, has been so completely metamorphosed as to be well nigh unrecognisable to the older generation. The youngster of today is born into a Bentley which his parents have seen created around them, a place which his grandfather never dreamed of'.

The Druids Arms public house on Bentley High Street. The pub can be traced back to at least 1841 and was rebuilt in 1906. Former owners have included W. Marsh, the Brook Hill Brewery Co., and Whitworth, Son & Nephew.

A tram passing along Bentley Road. In an article headed 'Bentley Trams to Go', the *Chronicle* of 16 October 1925 stated: 'The reconstruction of the road [along which the tram track ran] will necessitate an approximate expenditure of £21,000, towards which the Corporation has agreed to contribute £8,691, and the County Council the remainder. The roadway will be reconstructed in accordance with modern methods... Alterations to the overhead and electrical equipment of the line will cost £5,000... An extension of the existing route from the Bentley Village terminus, along the Avenue and Victoria Road, and thence in a southerly direction along the Doncaster and Selby main road is contemplated'.

Local photographer W. Scott has captured a scene at a church sale of work in the grounds of Bentley Vicarage on 13 August 1908. The event was opened by Lady Halifax. The object of the sale was to raise funds towards a new curate and a more adequate parish room. In a speech the vicar stated that due to the projected increase in population in the district he would need the asistance of a curate. Also, the parish room was far too small, and sometimes when he visited on a Sunday afternoon it was like the Black Hole of Calcutta.

Bentley's Infirmary Demonstration, c. June 1910, heading eastwards past the Druid's Arms public house. The event was held in J.H. Porrington's field. A large number of children from the various local schools were present and sang, conducted by C.P. Cowling, schoolmaster at the Bentley Council School.

This photograph shows the original Bentley High Street terminus which had a section of track leading into Chapel Street so that the trams would not obstruct other traffic in the main road. High Street is much the same today except for the plot of land behind the tram which is now the site of a new block of shops. The cottages at the bottom of the street have been replaced by a Catholic church; the spire of St Peter's church can just be seen behind one of the telegraph poles.

Bentley New Village Primary School, abutting on to Asquith Road, was opened on 2 January 1913. Mr W. Hinchcliff, as Chairman of the Bentley Education Sub-Committee, presided over the ceremony which was performed in one of the large assembly halls at the school. The West Riding County Council had bought the site from Messrs Barber, Walker & Co. The cost, including the site and building work, was over £10,000. Building operations commenced in September 1911, but the coal strike during the intervening period delayed the work some weeks.

Bentley Colliery under construction. Barber Walker & Company commenced a proving borehole near Bentley Mill in 1887, but owing to the nature of the strata bored through, the boring tackle fell into the borehole at a depth of 600 yards without proving the Barnsley Seam and the attempt was abandoned. In 1895 a further attempt was made by boring at the corner of Daw Lane Plantation and the rich Barnsley Seam was proved at a depth of 615 yards. Negotiations with local landowners for working rights followed and sinking was begun in 1904. This provided, in its initial stages, a striking example of indomitable courage and skill and the ultimate triumph over what seemed at one time to be insuperable difficulties. The triassic marls and sandstones in the area were overlain by 100 feet of quicksand which was encountered when only 8 ft of surface clay was passed through, so that the whole of the surface buildings had to be carried on huge concrete rafts. The great thickness of quicksand was unexpected for the borehole close to the shafts disclosed only 50 ft. The first attempt to penetrate the quicksand made by a sinking drum method of sinking was unsuccessful. It was then decided to adopt a method of sinking by a system of interlocking piles. The No. 2 shaft was the first to be commenced in 1905.

The sinking of the upcast shaft was started in October 1905 and a depth of 50 ft was reached in December of the same year. It was decided to sink through the quicksand - believed to be only 50 ft thick - by lowering bolted cast iron tubbing together with steel piles, grooved and tongued into each other, forming a complete circle round the outside of the bottom ring and sliding on the back of it. However, these operations proved unsuccessful and sinking was stopped, another attempt being made on 3 March 1906. The early days of Barnsley Seam coal working at Bentley have gone down in the history of mining, for the colliery became famous for experiments dealing with research into gob fires and spontaneous combustion.

On 6 November 1908 the *Doncaster Chronicle* noted: 'On Friday evening the pit sinkers at the Bentley Colliery were provided with dinner to celebrate the reaching of coal at both shafts, when there was an attendance of upwards of 300. The arrangements for the spread were admirably discharged by Mr Hildernby of the Bay Horse, Bentley, whose cuisine and general appointment met with the most cordial recognition. Dinner was served in a large marquee; lent by Messrs Cooper & Sons, Priory Place, erected in a field in Arksey Lane'.

After a *Chronicle* reporter had visted Bentley Colliery, he noted on 25 February 1910: 'The total employees of all grades at Bentley is now about 1,000 of whom some 700 are employed underground. The mine is worked in three shifts, and the output averages about 2,000 tons of coal per day... It is impossible to enjoy the privilege of a walk round without being impressed with the fact that everything one sees is of the latest and newest pattern; the mine is an absolutely first class one in every respect'.

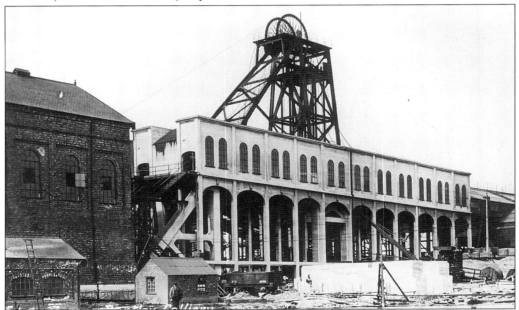

'When the first cartload of bricks was shot down early one morning in the place where the new Bentley now stands the lark was singing, the wild flowers were blooming upon the hedgerows, the rabbit and the fox lurked in the adjacent woods. This was about six years ago', reported the *Chronicle* on 25 February 1910. It also added: 'Now one can purchase picture postcards showing how complete is the transformation scene which has been effected in much less than a decade'.

View of Marsh's Mill, Bentley. John Marsh was noted as a miller in 1830.

View looking north east along The Avenue at Bentley. An idea of how the route appeared before building work took place is given by a *Chronicle* reporter on 25 February 1910: 'Through a little colony of new houses, colliers' cottages we passed on to a fine new broad road, still in the making. This road leads right to the pit and it is intended to extend the tram track here. Doubtless the road will, in a very few years time, have terrace houses the whole length of it. But, today there are fields to the right and left, overhead the birds are singing merrily'.

Two trams pass on a loop near Albion Terrace, Bentley Road. Opposite on the left is Bentley Rise. The *Chronicle* of 2 May 1913 stated: 'There is hardly a week passes but what a gang of men are to be seen repairing the tram track [at Bentley] and yet, in spite of all their labours, the Bentley route remains the worst of any on the whole system'.

Another view near Albion Terrace, Bentley Road, featuring car No. 7, purchased by Doncaster Corporation in 1902, fitted with a top deck in 1913 and withdrawn from service in 1930. On 21 September 1911 the *Chronicle* noted that the Bentley Urban District Council had recommended that the attention of the Doncaster Corporation be called to the serious overcrowding of the Bentley trams.

The extension of the Bentley tram route to near the colliery in 1924 was one of the last additions to the Doncaster network. Having just left the 'outer' terminus, car No. 24, purchased with five other tram cars in 1904, has been photographed by local camera man Luke Bagshaw on the 'passing loop' near the junction of The Avenue and Arksey Lane.

Car No. 6 has just crossed over the Great Central and Great Northern railway bridge at Bentley. The passing loop at this point was built around 1909. Much of the original track on the Bentley route was replaced during the First World War. Later, when road improvements were needed Doncaster Corporation refused to disturb the tracks again, deciding instead, during 1923, to replace the Bentley trams with trolleybuses, though this did not occur until 1928.

This picture was taken looking north from just past St Peter's church, Bentley; none of the cottages depicted here survive today.

J. Cooper's shop on Askern Road at Bentley Toll Bar. On 9 August 1912 the *Chronicle* reported: 'Bentley continues to grow more and more every day and yet the cry of the people continues to be "there are not sufficient houses"... The chief scene of building operations is on what is known as the 'Toll Bar Estate', where, just now there is a fair sized village in existence with a population of close upon a thousand. Three years ago there was one house on the the site, an old-fashioned toll-bar house. Up to the present there are 177 houses erected, including several shops, while the houses contemplated are more easily numbered in hundreds'.

The rebuilt Druids Arms public house on High Street, Bentley. Over the years the licensees of the pubs have included James Dodgson, Thomas Dodgson, William Skinner and Arthur Marshall.

The Railway Tavern in Cooke Street, Bentley, can be traced back to at least 1861 when William Holmes was the landlord. Former owners have included a Mrs J.C. Palmer. Pictured in the doorway is ex-licensee of the premises, Cyril Nokes.

Initially, Bentley's pleasure palace, known as the Coliseum, was something more than a cinematograph hall, having provision for staging variety and dramatic entertainments, as well as the latest productions in motion pictures. On opening in 1914 the *Gazette* of 4 September noted the following details: 'The auditorium is on a two tier principle and has comfortable seating accommodation for about 1,400 people. On the ground floor, which is on about the same level as the foyer, are the orchestra stalls, pit stalls, and pit. There are 500 tip-up chairs, upholstered in plush, in the orchestra stall, tip-up upholstered seats to the number of 300 in the pit stalls, and seating accommodation for about 350 in the pit. The circle comprises the second floor, and holds 500 tip-up chairs upholstered in red plush'.

Work on the Doncaster Co-operative Society's new store at the junction of High Street with Mill Gate began in October 1921 when the foundation stones were laid. The architects were Messrs Co-operative Wholesale Society Ltd, Architect's Department of Manchester, and the work was executed under their supervision by the building department of the same society.

Two views looking north on The Avenue, Bentley, with the tram track leading to the colliery. At a meeting held during November 1909, the ratepayers of Bentley-with-Arksey decided to apply to the county council for urban powers so that they could govern their own affairs. It was argued that since the opening of the colliery the population had gone up in leaps and bounds and the inhabitants were anxious for home rule. At that time they were under the control of the Doncaster District Council, who the Bentley residents said, did not look after Bentley properly and did not give them a proper return for the money they had to pay to the council.

The church of St Peter was erected in 1891 at a cost of £10,000, defrayed by the late Charles Edward Stephen Cooke esq. of St Catherine's, Doncaster. It is an edifice of stone in the Early English style from designs by J. Codd, architect, of London. The spire rises to a height of 120 ft and the church itself consists of chancel, nave, north and south porches, vestries and a tower. The church can seat 500, and the arms of the Cooke family can be seen inside. Bryan Cooke built the almshouses at Arksey for twelve poor people in 1660. The Endowed School at Arksey was built by Sir George Cooke in 1661.

A member of the Massarella family on one of his carts at Bentley.

Toll Bar takes its name from the old tollhouse which still stands. On 9 August 1912, the *Chronicle* noted: 'Houses in the [Bentley Toll Bar] district are principally occupied by colliers, who are employed at Carcroft and Bentley and sinkers at Askern. They are let at rentals varying between 6s 6d and 7s 6d per week, and are in such demand that even when the foundations are being sunk, even when the top soil is being taken off, would-be tenants go and see the landlord and deposit a week's rent in order to have the house. With the houses are coming the shops, and there are several big shops there already catering for various customers'.

A Bentley tram passes along Arksey Lane near the junction with The Avenue. The extension of the Bentley tram route to near the colliery in 1924 was one of the last additions to the Doncaster network. The commercial premises on the right, one section of which was erected in 1911, belong to a number of traders including Whitakers and Fred Pickersgill.

Watchhouse Lane, Bentley.

A Bentley tram pictured at the junction with High Street and Chapel Street. The Methodist chapel may be seen on the right along with the Bay Horse public house in the distance. The latter premises may be traced back to at least 1831. When the High Street was flooded in 1913 the *Chronicle* of 2 May commented: 'Not only have the pedestrians to suffer and go about in dread of being splashed with mud from passing vehicles, but the ride on the tram cars is almost as sensational as riding on the switchback'.

Children posing outside the Baptist church at Bentley, with Shakespeare Road on the right. The foundation stone was laid at the church by Mrs Ben Smith of Bradford on 30 September 1915. The building was opened 6 months later on 30 March 1916. With furniture, the cost was believed to be around £1,600 exclusive of the site. The architect was Herbert E. Illingworth ARIBA of Leeds and Harrogate.

A fine array of hats bobbing up and down on a sea of individuals at Bentley's Infirmary Demonstration. The picture was probably taken on Sunday 2 June 1910 in J.H. Porrington's field. Owing to bad weather the event had been postponed from the previous Sunday. Fortunately the weather on this occasion was fine and a large gathering assembled.

Bentley butcher William Pearson's horse and van is seen while out around the district on deliveries. His business premises were on Askern Road.

A man and his trusty steed pictured outside the Railway Hotel, Bentley. The premises underwent alterations during 1913.

The gaily painted carts of Bentley ice cream man Lewis Massarella can be seen here.

The Doncaster detachment of the 5th Battalion KOYLI attended the morning service at St Peter's church, Bentley, on Sunday 10 July 1910. They paraded at headquarters at 10.15 am and marched out headed by the band. Captain F.L. Parkin was in command. The company was well represented. The service was conducted by the vicar, the Revd A.E.B. Wade who preached about 'prayer' and pointed out that some of the greatest men had been those of constant prayer. He gave the Territorials a hearty welcome and said he always looked forward to them going to Bentley once a year, and when they failed he thought there was something missing.

The Bentley Toll Bar Club and Institute which was established in a nineteenth century toll cottage.

The Wesleyan Methodist chapel and Sunday schools on Chapel Street, Bentley, were erected in 1892 at a cost of £2,200; they were of red brick with stone dressings in the Gothic style. The chapel seated 365 persons and the schools held 200 children. The building has since been demolished.

st.25 Drinking Fountain M.W.Park.Bentley.JS&S.

View in Bentley Park. In July 1911, F. Kirkby, the Chairman of the Bentley Urban District Council received a letter on behalf of Mrs Ellen Walker, formerly of Conisborough, stating that she wished to present about 20 acres of land to the council as a park and recreation ground. The land was situated on Common Lane near the centre of the old part of Bentley. The council decided unanimously to accept the offer.

View in Bentley Park. Extensions were made to the park in 1924 and formally opened by the Minister of Mines, E. Shinwell. The extensions included a bowling green, three grass tennis courts, a golf putting green and an ornamental rock garden in addition to various children's activities such as a sand corner and paddling pool.

Children pose for the camera on a Bentley Bridge, *c*. 1910.

View in Bentley Park, *c*. 1930.

The Bentley Hotel in Watch House Lane was opened by Messrs J. Smith & Sons of Tadcaster in October 1913. With the gardens, a couple of full-sized bowling greens and the like, the hotel covered an area of 13,200 square yards, while the total cost was about £9,000. The architects were Messrs Bromit & Thorman and the contractors Messrs Mullins & Richardson of Doncaster. The first landlord was a Mr Hutton. Giving details of the interior layout the *Chronicle* of 10 October 1913 stated: 'The ground floor is given entirely up to hotel purposes, there being a music room 47 ft by 27 ft, capable of seating 300, a billiard room with two full-sized tables, a commercial room 18 ft by 19 ft... The interior walls and floors are of Italian Turazo work, the furnishing is on an elaborate style. The outside walls are of green glazed Saience bricks on the first floor, and rough casted Derbyshire Spar. Throughout the building is heated with radiators and hot water pipes, and lighted partly with electric and partly with gas'.

Watch House Lane with the Bentley Hotel on the right.

The post office on Bentley High Street which is still extant today. The house on the left has undergone alterations since the picture was taken. On 22 August 1930 the *Chronicle* announced that the Heap family had been sub-postmasters at Bentley for fifty years. 'William Heap was appointed sub-postmaster at Bentley on 15 August 1880, when the office was combined with that of beer off licence in Cook Street, next to the Bentley mill stream... but the post office business has extended so much that separate premises had to be taken in High Street nearly 30 years ago'. It is interesting to note that more than fifty years ago, the Bentley Post Office occupied a site at the junction of Mill Gate and High Street, where the Co-operative Stores now stand.

The Doncaster Mutual Co-operative and Industrial Society's store at the corner of High Street and Mill Gate, Bentley.

Broughton Avenue, looking towards houses being built on Watchhouse Lane. The shop on the right, at the corner of Stockbridge Avenue, is presently occupied by hairdresser Mr Todz. At one time the Broughtons were well known in Bentley. They were a very old family and can trace their record in Arksey church register for 400 years. It was a Mrs Broughton, wife of the late Joshua Broughton, who presented St Peter's church with a peal of bells.

Bentley Road looking towards Doncaster. Grove House is on the immediate left and the two women are standing outside No. 313 Bentley Road.

Brookside, Bentley, featuring Yew Tree Farm on Askern Road. Since the view was taken the area has been redeveloped and a health centre occupies part of the site.

A photograph showing Bentley miners posing in Elm Crescent during the 1926 General Strike while preparing food for a soup kitchen located nearby.

In 1913 the parents of children living at Bentley Toll Bar considered they were not properly treated and did not obtain adequate return for payment of rates in the form of elementary school accommodation. So they decided, by a large majority, to keep their children away from school until such time as the authorities built a temporary school. One of the pictures here shows a policeman gathering those children who were willing to go to school. He escorted them there and home again at night. In September 1914, a junior and infants school was opened at Toll Bar. The photograph of the policeman with the group of children was taken at the junction of Askern Road and Ansdell Road.

The most disastrous floods in living memory inundated the Doncaster district during May 1932. Following 30 hours continuous rainfall, starting on 20 May, millions of gallons of water swept down the Don Valley. Rivers overflowed their banks with little or no warning and thousands of people were rendered homeless. Hundreds of acres of land were underwater, while villages were cut off and many farmsteads and houses completely isolated. The loss to farmers, householders and local authorities was immense. The *Gazette* of 27 May 1932 said: 'Surely the most tragic village in England must be Bentley. Within nine months it has twice been overwhelmed by floods and it was only last November that the terrible pit disaster there shocked the whole country'.

The lonely out-post."
...holme Square, Bentley during Floods.

As the water increased on Monday 23 May, the horses found it increasingly difficult to make their way through it. The carts began to sway ominously and it was decided to rush boats to the scene. With the water still rising on Tuesday, the people who had remained in their homes spent a night of terror. In the main road the water reached a depth of 6 ft and in some of the houses in the side roads it was 9 and 10 ft deep.

...aw Lane during Floods at Bentley.   "Empire View" 57

"Flood Reflections".
Dove Lane, Bentley during Floods.

"Empire View." 55.

Bentley Toll Bar, where almost 10 ft of water stood in the houses, suffered most from the floods, and relief measures were carried out. So serious was the position that government officials made an extensive tour of the area.

Grange Road, Toll Bar, Bentley during Floods.

"Empire View." 57.

At the first signs of the flood, Bentley Toll Bar people made preparations and moved everything possible into the rooms upstairs. The houses in the streets leading off the main road were flooded to a depth of 4 ft before there was much water on the main road. The people were at first somewhat reluctant to leave their homes, but as the water continued to rise they realised the seriousness of the position. Bentley Council soon had a number of carts and drays drawn by horses to bring the people out of the marooned houses and take others to and fro.

Arthur Street, Bentley, flood-bound.

...ned by Floods.

Draining down from other areas the water rushed into Toll Bar on Tuesday evening and rose rapidly. It rushed up the Askern Road beyond Bentley Moor Lane; both Adwick Lane and Bentley Moor Lane, below, were flooded and became impassable.

7. YARBOROUGH TERRACE, DONCASTER DURING FLOODS...

"Swirling Rapids" Floods at Hunt Lane, Bentley, Doncaster. May 1932. View 29.

Despite the floods tradesmen carried on bravely as long as they could. The people marooned in their houses required provisions, but finally had to fetch what they could when they were able to get to dry land by means of the boats and carts. It was stated that the council was already overburdened with debt and it would be necessary to keep the expenses incurred by the floods to a minimum. It was costing the council about £4 a day to deliver fresh water and food by boats to those who had stayed in their homes.

Askern Road, Toll Bar, Bentley and Schools during Floods. "Empire View". 50.

Over 1,000 people in the Bentley district were seriously affected by the floods. A week after the rain first appeared, thousands were still homeless and nearly 500 people were accommodated in the New Village school. A difficult position arose when the people in the school resented being treated on institutional lines and the West Riding County Council had to withdraw the arrangements they had made for providing food and other necessities.

In addition to forty boats there was also a motor boat. Rafts, which were being used on the Askern Road, were withdrawn and people were rescued in horse vehicles. There were also a number of sick people saved and instances where the invalids were carried half a mile on stretchers mounted on the shoulders of the wading bearers. Colonel Pickering and a Mr C. Jackson of the British area of the British Legion were authorised by the London headquarters to give £100 from the Legion funds to the Bentley Flood Disaster Fund.

The Bentley mining community pay their last respects to the forty-five men and boys killed in the underground explosion at the colliery disaster on 20 November 1931. The disaster had not only horrified Bentley people, but met with nationwide sympathy. Fortunately, the unique ventilation system isolated the outburst to one district, or the disaster, in human terms, might have been greater.

The great work in the 1932 floods was in evacuating the families living at Toll Bar. This task necessitated the people getting into the boats with a few articles of bedding and being rowed a distance of three-quarters of a mile, where they had to land, then walk over a long railway bridge which carries the the main road to Selby to board a raft on the other side, to be carried a further third of a mile to a landing stage.

Doncaster's first operational trolley service ran on the Bentley route on 22 August 1928. A trolleybus journey to and from Bentley took 30 minutes. Usually five trolleybuses operated on this route, with six on Saturdays.

RT. HON. DONCASTER JOSSE.
(ORIGINALLY KNOWN AS BENTLEY JOSSE)

Bentley Joss, as his name suggests, was a local Bentley character. Of all the quaint, colourful characters ever associated with Doncaster and district, not one was more widely known or more popular than the man whose only home was a ramshackle wooden shack secluded in a woodland strip down Brustlingholme Lane (now perhaps aptly renamed Jossey Lane). He always wore a square-topped mortar-board college cap, black cravat and plus fours hanging loosely at his ankles. Over his shoulder he carried a stick shaped much like a shortened billiards cue. Rumour had it that his real name was Fowler and it was popularly believed that he was connected with one of the county families, being a cast-off love child.

On leaving the town centre depot, before commencing services near the Brown Cow public house on North Bridge, Bentley trolleybuses travelled via French Gate, St Sepulchre Gate, Station Road and Trafford Street. Trolleybus No. 35 is pictured here.

The Bentley trolleybuses did not terminate near the Bentley Colliery Workmen's Club and Institute as the trams had done previously. They continued along The Avenue, turned left along Victoria Road and back to Playfairs Corner via Askern Road. However, it was discovered that most passengers used the service between the town centre and Playfairs Corner. Therefore any 'special' trolleybuses operating on the Bentley route on Saturdays or at busy times during the week, relieved those travelling on the 'normal' route by terminating and turning round at Playfairs Corner - like the trolleybus pictured here.

Four
Carcroft and Bullcroft Colliery

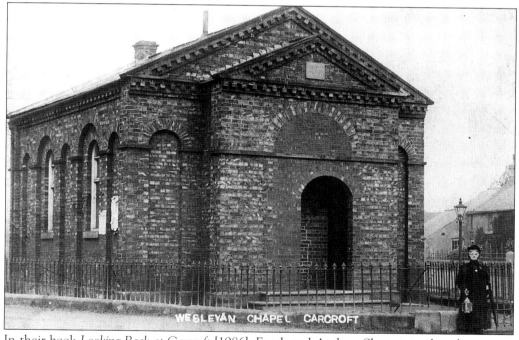

In their book *Looking Back at Carcroft* [1986], Frank and Andrew Shaw state that the woman depicted holding a lantern is thought to be a Mrs Oates, worshippers needing to take their own lighting in order to read the service books. Later on, the chapel, at the junction of Skellow Road and Chestnut Avenue (Pickhill Lane), was used as a garage, a fish and chip shop, a barbers shop and Dick Smith's general store.

High Street, Carcroft, the new brick-built shops at the centre of the picture being erected by 'Turp' Ogden. The properties on either side of the new building have since been demolished, the transformation of the area gathering momentum in the years before the First World War.

The old Wesleyan chapel, off-centre left, and the former Carcroft Village Club and Institute, to the right, are featured here. The opening of the club and institute was mentioned in the *Chronicle* of 18 November 1910: 'The idea of forming the institution was mooted about the commencement of May last by six persons. They called a meeting which took place on May 21st, when it was decided to form a club. An old barn exactly opposite the the Bullcroft Colliery yard and belonging to Mr Clark, a farmer, was obtained on a five year lease... there is at present a membership of 104, including three local doctors and the Vicar of of the Parish, the Rev. J.C. Brockwell'.

Grocery and provisions merchant Alf Dennis' shop on West View, Carcroft. While sinking problems were being overcome at Bullcroft, the *Chronicle* of 20 May 1910, noted that a number of land surveyors and their assistants were busy mapping out further developments at Carcroft. Notice boards were prominently displayed in green fields announcing 'eligible plots for sale'.

This is how a section of Carcroft High Street appeared before the alterations, seen on the previous page, occurred. The same view is unrecognisable today, all the buildings depicted having been cleared. Noting the changes in the area the *Chronicle* of 16 May 1913 reported: 'At the present moment there are about 1,800 hands employed at the pit, largely drawn from the mining districts of Derbyshire and Nottinghamshire... Houses are springing up like mushrooms, there are rows and rows and rows of houses, some of them laid out in the form of a model village and the old rural population is completely swamped by the mining element'.

The post office on Skellow Road. The Bullcroft Colliery entrance gates and offices are adjacent on the right. Of the pit's position the *Chronicle* of 20 May 1910 noted: 'Like the other pits [in the South Yorkshire coalfield] Bullcroft is charmingly situated, so far as its natural surroundings are concerned. It lies in the midst of green fields, yet it is within a few yards of the roadway on the one hand and the railway on the other'.

The corner of Owston Road and High Street, Carcroft. The latter was completely altered after production commenced at Bullcroft Colliery. The shops on the left were built around 1913, their occupants at the time the picture was taken included Gallon (general dealer), G. Booker and W. Beresford.

General dealer and chemist W. Bytheway's store on Park Avenue, Carcroft. Around the turn of the century there were only forty or fifty houses in the village. By 1910 this had increased to around 400, many of these being red brick buildings.

Bentley Moor Road, Carcroft, in the early stages of completion. The *Chronicle* of 16 May 1913 mentioned that in many respects most of the miners' houses at Carcroft, Owston and Skellow, set an example to colliers' homes in other parts, even of the Doncaster district: 'They are larger and roomy, almost every house has its bath, its hot and cold water, and its w.c. The streets for the most part are wide and spacious, and in contrast to the grimy and monotonous villages on the other side of Doncaster, the place around Bullcroft Colliery makes a little paradise'.

Looking east along Lodge Road with Markham Avenue on the right. Some of the Markham Avenue houses were supposedly built around 1911 to accommodate Bullcroft pit officials. The Colliery Company were the owners of a large part of land below Owston Park and in order to encourage their employees at Bullcroft to become owners of their own houses, and thus feel they had a more permanent interest in the locality, they made special terms whereby any man who so desired could become owner of his little home.

Carcroft Club, erected in 1914, on Chestnut Avenue. These premises have since been replaced by a new building, opened in recent years.

J. Hill (right) was formerly a landlord of the Moon Inn, Carcroft. The picture was taken in his farmyard with son Frankie proudly posing in the small wagon. In Carcroft there was little change or growth for perhaps 400 years until coal was discovered. With this discovery many of the traditions of the old farming community were destroyed.

Carcroft Peace celebrations in 1919, featuring Harry Rylands (left) in his soldier/bride costume, aproaching Gallons Corner from Owston Road. The *Chronicle* of 25 July 1919 stated that Carcroft had an outstanding Peace pageant. 'On every hand there was abundant enthusiasm over the proceedings, on every hand there was enough and to spare in the way of food and sport, and finally there was quite a small army of willing helpers eager and ready to do anything to assist in the success of the day'.

Two views taken at different times, but from nearly the same standpoint on Owston Road, Carcroft. The thoroughfare is still a hive of commercial activity today.

These shops were obviously built to serve the needs of the miners and their families. The Bullcroft enterprise was one of the Markham group of collieries that were built around Doncaster during the early years of the century. The Bullcroft coal was beneath the estates of Major Anne, (Burghwallis Hall), Mr Cooke-Yarborough (Compsmount) and other local landowners.

The Provident Stores in the centre of the picture was erected in 1913, becoming known in later years as 'The Thrift'.

Skellow Road, Carcroft, looking west, where trees and fields no longer form a part of the view.

The above picture shows housebuilding for colliers at Carcroft. The *Chronicle* of 6 September 1912 mentioned that, partly with the idea of providing accommodation for the miners near the Bullcroft Colliery, and partly to prevent the place becoming an eye-sore, such as many mining places were, the Colliery Company was erecting a model village at Carcroft. 'The site chosen is in Corpse Lane [now Owston Road], Carcroft, in the shadow of Owston Park, and overlooking the colliery. Plans for 148 houses have been approved by the Doncaster RDC and one half of these will be erected as soon as possible'.

A view taken from the top of Paddy Bridge, Carcroft. Mary Green (née Wood) is holding the horse and Beattie Emmons is standing in the cart.

Aerial view of Carcroft, featuring from left to right, Markham Avenue, Owston Road, Paxton Avenue and New Street.

Aerial view of Carcroft looking north west with Bullcroft Colliery dominating the foreground. Skellow Road cuts across the top right corner. The sinking of Bullcroft Colliery commenced in November 1909, and the Barnsley Seam was reached in December 1911. Owing to the soft nature of the water-bearing limestone measures it was decided to sink two shafts. Yet, due to the large feeder of water amounting at one time to 8,000 gallons per minute, it was impossible to get enough pumps into the shaft to deal with it and carry on sinking. In addition, the water was washing away the soft limestone between the two shafts and endangering the surface buildings by subsidence. For these reasons it was decided to allow the shaft to fill with water and freeze. The contract was let to the Shaft Freezing Co. Ltd of Great Britain, an offshoot of a German firm. A Mr Gebhardt was chief engineer and the engineer in charge was a Mr Dutz. After boring operations were completed and the freezing of the strata commenced, it was found that water was circulating and running out at the pit top, preventing a complete ice wall being formed. To stop this the tubbing was continued above ground level at a height of 15 ft. The water came to rest about 6 ft above ground level. The ice wall then quickly formed and sinking through the frozen ground commenced.

Group in the doorway of Carcroft Wesleyan chapel, which has since become the premises of Murten's Joinery Co.

A VE party at the rear of the houses on Askern Road, Carcroft.

The Picture House at Carcroft, designed by Blythe Richardson of Doncaster, opened in 1924; the building survived until 1992 when it was demolished.

Two views of the Moon Inn, High Street, Carcroft, which can be traced back to at least 1814. Over the years it may also have been known as the 'Half Moon' and during 1861 and 1877 was noted as the 'Sun'. Its former owners have included Philip Bryan Davies Cooke of Owston Hall. The pub is shown in both views before alterations and extensions in 1910.

Posing proudly outside the Moon Inn on 15 July 1923, are collectors for the Carcroft and District Hospital Demonstration.

A New Moon Hotel was designed by John Smith's Brewery architect B. Wilson, and erected by B. Groves of Goldthorpe, on the site seen here at the junction of Skellow Road and High Street. Part of the old Moon was once occupied by Northern Upholstery.

Scene at Bullcroft Colliery in 1912. It was mentioned in the *Chronicle* of 16 May 1913 that all the employees at Bullcroft Colliery engaged in the manipulation of coal, both underground and on the surface, numbering in all about 1,800, have to become trade unionists. The usual procedure of stopping the contributions from the wage was carried out. 'This method of procedure is becoming more and more favourable to the officials of the Union, and if the fight for unionism becomes general throughout Yorkshire, as a result of the agitation that is at present going on, this method will no doubt become general'.

Bullcroft Colliery, Carcroft. By 1913 it was being reported that since the initial sinking problems, the whole scene at Bullcroft was going like clockwork. 'The shaft was sunk to the coal measures, winding gears and the pit head apparatus were erected, and for the past 15 months coal has been drawn out from the workings, 680 yards below. The output at the colliery averages 18,000 tons per week'.

Slackwasher at Bullcroft Colliery, Carcroft. The *Chronicle* of 14 December 1911 stated: 'Since the sinking commenced there has not been a single serious accident - all the more remarkable bearing in mind the unexampled danger and difficulty of dealing with the water problem. The managing director of the mine is Mr Humble and the engineer, Mr De Seifreyd, a brilliant young Pole, since whose coming the work has proceeded without a hitch'.

Miners posing at Bullcroft Colliery, Carcroft, in 1912. On Saturday 8 December 1911, the countryside around Carcroft had been stirred by the strident calls of half a dozen buzzers. It was the means devised to announce the fact that coal had at last been reached at the Bullcroft Colliery sinkings, at a depth of 657 yds.

Laying the 'loop' line for Bullcroft Colliery.

The electric lamp room at Bullcroft Colliery.

Miners at Bullcroft Colliery, Carcroft in 1912. In the early stages of the pit's operation the Colliery Company recognised that the miner was always an enthusiastic lover of sports and lent its support to the Sports and Pastime's Association. This was for the benefit of all the employees and each of them contributed an amount per week towards providing various kinds of sports.

Miners at Bullcroft Colliery. On 31 August 1961 the *Gazette* revealed that for almost twenty years, mining engineers throughout the world had been interested in Bullcroft Colliery. This was because the pit was still demonstrating the method pioneered in the early days of the Second World War of preventing spontaneous combustion in the waste behind the coal face. 'The mixture of hard and soft coal in the [Barnsley] seam made the colliiery one of the most vulnerable to spontaneous combustion'.

Albert Middleton and Bernard
Hutchinson at Bullcroft Colliery.

Miners at Bullcroft Colliery, 1944.

Miners at Bullcroft Colliery, 1944. The pit closed in the early 1970s, miners being absorbed into
the nearby Brodsworth pit and the NCB workshops in Carcroft. The *Gazette* of 17 September
1970 gave the following details: 'The merger [set for Monday 28 September] will mean the
closure of two of the three Bullcroft seams and the third will be worked from Brodsworth. In the
merger only 40 men will be made redundant, all of them are over the age of 60 and almost 700
men will undertake the move from Bullcroft'.

Five

Woodlands and Brodsworth Colliery

The Woodlands Hotel on the Great North Road was built in 1914 by the People's Refreshment House Association Ltd. This group was formed in 1896 by a number of Temperance reformers. Their aims included 'the encouragement of temperance by reform in the management of licensed inns, public houses and canteens' and 'the provision of facilities for the prompt supply of food and non-alcoholic refreshment at licensed houses not merely drinking bars'. Subsequent owners of the hotel included Ind Coope and Allsopp Ltd. The Woodlands Hotel was demolished after suffering fire damage in the early hours of Saturday 4 February 1989. A new, smaller hotel has since been erected on the site.

On 23 October 1905, a group of people assembled in a Pickburn field on the Brodsworth Estate. They were there to witness the cutting of the first sod at Brodsworth Colliery by Brodsworth Estate owner Charles Thellusson. This would mark the beginning of an undertaking destined to

provide employment for over 3,000 men, to yield to the nation many millions of tons of highest grade coal and to result in the creation of a colliery and village.

Miller (1804) notes that Woodlands, in the parish of Adwick, was built by Thomas Bradford, who sold it, with a small quantity of adjoining land, to Christopher Waterton. Regarding the house's name, Gordon Smith in the *Gazette* of 13 January 1966, records that this small mansion was sometimes known as Woodlands Hall though it is properly called The Woodlands, adding: 'Although the architecture of this house, is not in the highest classical taste, it is well proportioned, being built of red brick (now covered white) the centre block being headed by a three-bay pediment. The ground floor possesses two large stone-bay windows, which appear to have been a larger addition'. During the present century, The Woodlands has become the Park Club.

General view of the cutting of the first sod at Brodsworth Main Colliery on 23 October 1905. Until the early part of this century, the mining operations on the great South Yorkshire Coalfield had been confined to the planting of collieries on the outcrop of the coal measures extending from Conisborough to Penistone. Owing to the exhaustion of the principal profitable coal seams at the comparatively shallow depths in that neighbourhood, it became necessary to carry on operations by deeper sinkings to the east. Brodsworth was an example of this.

Brodsworth Main Colliery. The shafts were deepened to the Parkgate Seam commencing in 1920. The seam was reached in December 1921, at a depth of 814 yards. It was 4 ft 7 in thick with a rock roof and strong stone floor. The shaft sides were secured with brick lining. Number 3 shaft was commenced in 1923 and reached the Barnsley Seam, which was its limit, in July 1924.

Brodsworth Main Colliery, described in the *Chronicle* of 15 April 1910, as 'a dirty picture in a golden frame. The pit is the picture, the frame is the delightful countryside, the really rural and rustic surroundings by which the pit is enclosed. For here we have countryside and commercialism in all conscience. Within a few feet of the colliery pay office is a green field, and in this stands a haystack'.

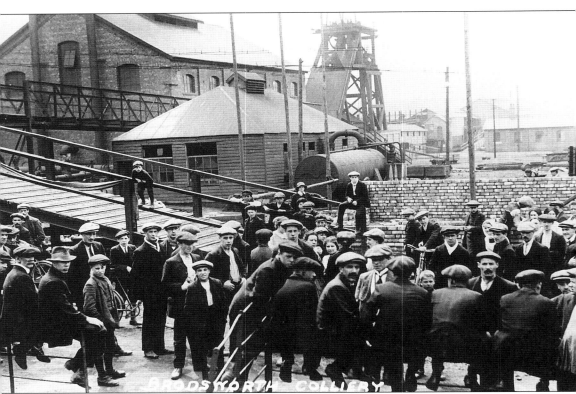

Miners at Brodsworth Main Colliery

Particulars about colliers' wages were given in the *Gazette* of 7 August 1914: 'Those of the surfacemen varied from 24s, or 25s up to £2 a week, and down the pit they received from 7s 6d a day in some cases a little less or just under £2 a week, up to £3 a week. About 20 per cent of the men were surfacemen. During the last eighteen months the colliery had employed 200 to 300 more men, about 2,500 being employed at the present time'.

Engine House, Brodsworth Colliery. The *Chronicle* of 15 April 1910 noted that, with the exception of the downcast engine house and two huge chimney stacks, the pit head frames and the whole of the colliery buildings are constructed of wood. 'At the commencement of operations it was decided to take out the shaft pillars, and allow the ground to settle. But when coal was found at a less depth than was expected, the pillars were allowed to remain. The down cast engine house was built at a later date'.

Brodsworth Colliery was formerly the joint property of the Hickleton Main Colliery Co. Ltd and the Stavely Coal and Iron Co. Ltd. It was served by three railways, the Hull & Barnsley, the Great Northern, and the Great Central, being situated some 2 miles from Adwick and Carcroft station.

Formal group at Brodsworth Colliery.

Formal group at Brodsworth Colliery.

Formal group at Brodsworth Colliery.

Formal group at Brodsworth Main Fire Station.

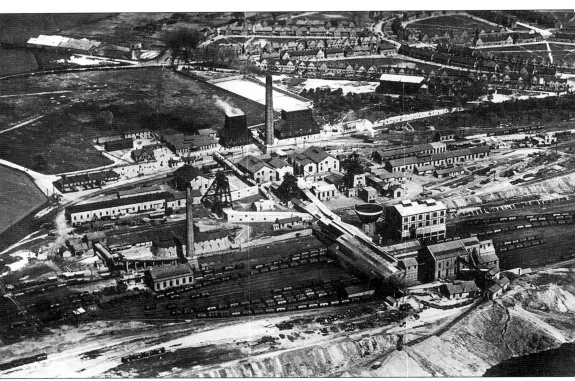

Aerial view of Brodsworth Colliery.

Tram terminus at Woodlands, adjacent to the main road and opposite Windmill Balk Lane.
The Brodsworth tram route was so called because it was mainly intended to serve Brodsworth
Colliery. However, the route terminated in Woodlands and passengers travelling to the colliery
had to walk the remainder of the journey.

Post office at Woodlands.

Wesleyan chapel at Woodlands. 'At the beginning of the twentieth century Methodism made a vigorous and successful bid to mission the coalmining villages that sprang up around Doncaster. In 1913 a committee was established with representatives from the Wesleyan Methodists and Primitive Methodists to discuss "preventing overlapping and arranging for better distribution of service" in the South Yorkshire Coalfield' wrote Geoffrey Morris in *The Story of Methodism in Doncaster and District 1743-1988* (published 1988).

North Road Market, Woodlands.

The Great North Road Market at Woodlands. Amongst the traders were J. Potts jnr (motorcycles), J.W. Johnson (boot repairer), E. Pickering (hairdresser) and Millard's (jewellers).

The first part of the Woodlands Model Village to be developed - known as The Park - contained 121 cottages, at a density of five to the acre, overlooking a 24 acre green, surounded by well established trees. At several points the line of the buildings was set back in order to preserve a large tree and the houses were grouped round them.

Entrance to Model Village, Woodlands: an example of a private village built expressly to house the people working for a colliery. It was designed by Chesterfield architect Percy Houfton during 1907-8. Dr McKay's and Dr Ashforth's first surgery in Woodlands is on the right. Mr John Dill, an official at the pit, lived to the left.

First Avenue, Woodlands. The *Chronicle* of 15 April 1910 stated that the Woodlands cottages are picturesque and of varied design, and did not at all suggest a colliery village. 'There are five types of houses, the rents of which vary from 5s 6d per week to 6s 3d. For the most part, the exterior of the dwellings is of white rough cast walls, with red gables and red tiled roofs, doors and window frames being painted a vivid green'.

View of The Crescent, Woodlands, with the church on the left. Woodlands was built in two phases and included primary and secondary schools, a Methodist chapel, Church of England place of worship, health centre and church hall. The community buildings were centrally situated to provide better education and a deeper sense of spiritual values.

The Park at Woodlands. The *Chronicle* [*op. cit.*] informed: 'The [Woodlands] houses are well equipped, and there is an amplitude of garden and air space. If the Brodsworth miner does not consider himself very fortunate in comparison with some of his class he must indeed be lacking in appreciation'.

The Great North Road at Woodlands looking north, with the Woodlands Hotel on the right. When the premises were owned by the People's Refreshment House Association Ltd, the resident licensed manager was paid a fixed salary and obtained no profit on alcoholic sales. However, they did receive a share of the profits from the sale of food and non-intoxicants and were bound by contract to supply these on request. Also, alcoholic drinks were not advertised in the association's houses, except on the necessary price lists.

Woodlands May Festival, 28 May 1910. The idea of holding the festival originated with Arthur J. Jay, headmaster of the Woodlands Provided School. The initial difficulties were largely surmounted by the generosity of C. Thellusson of Brodsworth Hall to guarantee the committee to the extent of £20. This enabled matters to progress. Further meetings were held and a number of sub-committees were appointed to provide for and arrange the very numerous details. Not least exacting was the fixing up of the costumes. This was really a colossal task and made great demands upon the resources and ingenuity of the committee responsible. A procession is seen here passing through the village.

THE WOODLANDS MAY FESTIVAL

When crowning the May Queen, Miss Cissie Robinson, on 28 May 1910, Miss Thellusson exclaimed: 'With this emblem of purity I deck thee; that all who bow before thee may know that honour, love, and faith are by thee held most dear. This sceptre, which signifies power, I pray thee accept, and while we thus place unlimited power in thy hands we know that it will be used for Justice and the Right. We crown thee Queen of the May. All around thee are loyal subjects and true, who will obey thy every wish and command. Hail to our Queen! The Queen of the May! Hail'.

Woodlands Festival, May 1910, showing the May Queen Miss Cissie Robinson, who had been elected to her proud position by the votes of her fellow schoolmates. She rode a beautiful white palfrey, with crimson trappings, kindly lent by the Rector of Adwick-le-Street, the Revd E.E. Farmer. The supreme act of crowning Cissie with flowers was gracefully performed by Miss Adeline Thellusson, representing Mrs Thellusson, who was with her husband in Sweden.

The Woodlands Festival, 28 May 1910. The procession, part of which is seen here, comprised 1,000 people, the greater percentage of whom were in fancy dress. Starting from the Mission Room at 1.30 pm and headed by the Woodlands Brass Band, it paraded all the principal roads of the village, ultimately marching to the grounds surrounding the Brodsworth Club.

Boy scout Charlie Steele poses with Winnie and Marion Dixon whilst appearing in one of the Woodlands Festivals.

A formal group showing Woodlands boy scouts, who regularly featured in the annual festivals at Woodlands.

Woodlands children going to Brodsworth Hall on 15 September 1910. These children, along with those from schools at Brodsworth, Adwick-le-Street, Marr and Hampole, were invited to the Hall to be included in the celebrations of the silver wedding of Mr and Mrs C. Thellusson. As the 1,350 beaming, happy youngsters marched across the terrace to be received by their hosts a most pleasing scene was formed.

The opening of the Doncaster Co-operative Society's stores at Woodlands on Saturday 1908. The ceremony was performed by Councillor Wightman JP, resident of the Doncaster Co-operative Society, supported by the Mayor of Doncaster Alderman J.F. Clark, F. Maddison MP, F. Hall MP, and others. Percy Houfton, of Chesterfield, was the architect and the building contract worth £3,500 was carried out by Messrs Mullins and Richardson of Doncaster. There were shops for grocery and provisions, fresh meat, fish and game, drapery, clothing, chemists, hairdressing and furniture. The shops were in the centre of the west side of the model village. They were lit up with acetylene gas, fitted by the Leading Light Syndicate, of Hull. The grocery department was fitted up with patent flour shoots by Messrs Hall and Kay.

Woodlands Festival showing a procession in The Crescent.

Carnival Day, Woodlands. Following a procession through the village, numerous events, for both adults and childreen and lasting well into the evening, were held in the grounds of Brodsworth Club. The *Doncaster Chronicle* of 3 June 1910 stated: 'There could surely be no more suitable spot for a May Day festival than the park-like grounds of Brodsworth Club. The delightful natural surroundings, the wealth of greenery and foliage, the shimmering lake extending away through the trees - the district is, indeed, appropriately named Woodlands. Amid these sylvan beauties the May revels took place'.

A close-up of participants in the Brodsworth (Woodlands?) May Festival.

Scene at Woodlands May Festival (date unknown).

Scene at Woodlands May Festival showing children round the maypole on 28 May 1910. On 3 June 1910, the *Chronicle* reported: 'The ode to the Maypole having been sung, the junior girls brought forward their Maypole with its pretty streamers. To suitable musical accompaniment they gave (1) the water wheel, (2) plait and, (3) spider's web. They also gave the national dances of the United Kingdom very neatly and prettily executed in each case'.

Tea party at Woodlands.

Scene at Woodlands Festival (date unknown).

The Woodlands Carnival of 13 July 1912 commenced in the Woodlands Club grounds. A large stage with a platform in front, which had been erected for the May Festival in 1911 was again made use of for the Queen of the Carnival and her court. This was naturally decorated with greenery and roses, the Queen's throne, seen here, being similarly adorned.

Woodlands Carnival, 13 July 1912, showing Lady Halifax crowning the Carnival Queen, Miss Gladys Bonsall. It was reported in the *Chronicle* of 19 July 1912 that upon the arrival of the procession the Queen of the Carnival, in beautiful white silk, alighted from her decorated car and, with her train carried by two pages and followed by her court, mounted the stage and stood with all her court around her while *Rule Britannia* was played by the band.

Scene at the Woodlands Carnival held on 13 July 1912, showing the Queen of the Carnival, Miss Gladys Bonsall, with her maids of honour. The *Chronicle* [*op. cit.*] gave the following details: 'Never has a Queen had a more brilliant court, nor a more representative one. Every colour and country appeared to have sent its representative. The court sat on a stage decked with greenery and roses, with the Queen seated in Royal state high up in their midst'.